Can you find...

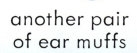

another pair
of ear muffs

5 more green
fir trees

2

3

Who else has found a juicy orange?

Spot the snow person without a hat.

Can you find...

2 different pairs of mittens

6 other blue buttons

4

5 more orange
carrot noses

1 different
bucket

3 shovels, all
different

Spot another bag like mine!

Who's hanging upside down?

Can you find... another pair of boots like this 1 spider with a different hat

6

3 other white chocolate mice

1 more flying bat

a sock that matches this one

Spot a squirrel on a snowboard!

2 more yellow flags

3 flying birds like this

1 more hot-air balloon

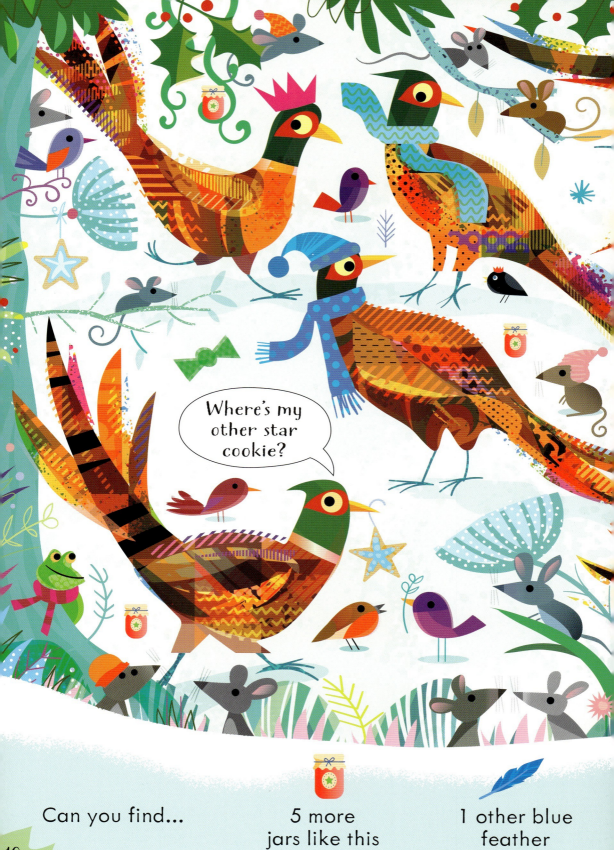

Can you find...

5 more
jars like this

1 other blue
feather

another pair
of boots like this

3 more
green bows

another 2
black birds

Who has a sack of presents?

another tiny snow person

1 more mouse-sized brush

2 more bird cookies

Can you find...

2 more rolls of pink paper

3 other fox-shaped cookies

14

3 more pairs
of scissors

2 other rolls
of red tape

another basket
of goodies

Who is reading a story?

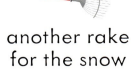
another rake
for the snow

1 more
bug in a rug

2 other cupcakes
like this

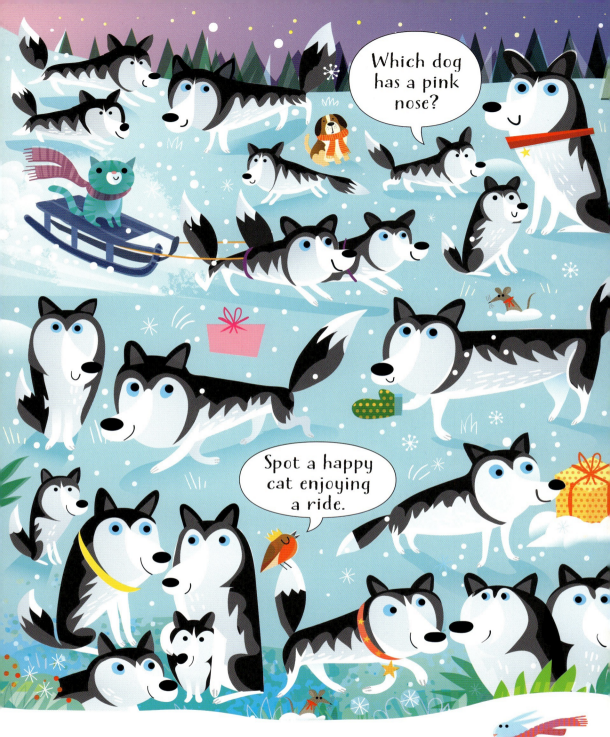

Can you find...

1 more gift for a dog

another rabbit just like this

1 more
little puppy

another 5
brown mice

1 more
tiny tree

Can you see six cherry cupcakes?

Hot Chocolate + Cakes

Can you find...

2 different party crowns

7 mugs that match this one

20

I spy a fox. Can you?

2 other pairs of red skates

1 more silver flute

another 2 hats like this

23

Find four blue knitted sweaters.

Which of us is upside down?

Can you find...

2 more letters

a different cheese-shaped gift

5 more
acorns

3 other burning
candles

4 different
candy canes

Whose scarf matches my socks?

Can you find...

2 other orange cats with hats

3 more golden bells

another little
snow hare

4 more footprints
like this

1 other pair
of toy antlers

Find a fox sitting on a box.

3 more red balloons

5 different bright balls

3 other socks like this

29

Answers

Cover

2–3

4–5

6–7

8–9

10–11

12–13

14–15

16–17

18–19

20–21

22–23

24–25

26–27

28–29

First published in 2023 by Usborne Publishing Ltd, Usborne House, 83-85 Saffron Hill, London, EC1N 8RT, England.
usborne.com © 2023 Usborne Publishing Ltd. The name Usborne and the Balloon logos are trade marks of Usborne Publishing Ltd. All rights reserved. No part of this publication may be reproduced, stored in a retrieval system, or transmitted in any form or by any means without the prior permission of the publisher.
UE. First published in America in 2023. Printed in China.